D1162069

York-Goldman Enterprises presents

Fun in the Sun Safely

Written by, **Dianne York-Goldman**

Illustrations by, **Lisa Notley**

Copyright ©2004 York-Goldman Enterprises, Inc.

Copyright ©2004 by York-Goldman Enterprises, Inc.

All rights reserved. Reproduction of the material herein
in any form requires the written permission of the publisher.

Publisher York-Goldman Enterprises, Inc.
Editor John Siebert
Text & Cover Design Aloha Graphic Design
Illustration Lisa Notley

ISBN# 0-9706688-1-3

York-Goldman Enterprises, Inc.

7630 Fay Avenue • La Jolla, California 92037 • tel: 858.456.2992 • web: www.youglowgirl.com

This book belongs to:

_____

A gift from:

_____

Meet my friends and my foes
Said the sun to the class,
Some harm your skin
While some help the grass.
But don't be confused
Because I have so many,
Let me explain
Dear Tommy and Jenny.

We'll start with my foes
My enemies and yours,
They're called ultraviolet rays
UV rays for short.
Though they do come from me
I'm not all bad.
They cause wrinkles and blotches
And cancers, so sad.
They're invisible criminals
That come from the sky,
They cause burns on your skin
And even your eye.

But a burn isn't all
You must watch for these days,
People can also
Get spots from my rays.
There are differences, though
In appearance and size,
And a doctor can show you
Where it is cancer lies.
In a mole that is dark
And continues to grow,
That is the one
You should look for and show.

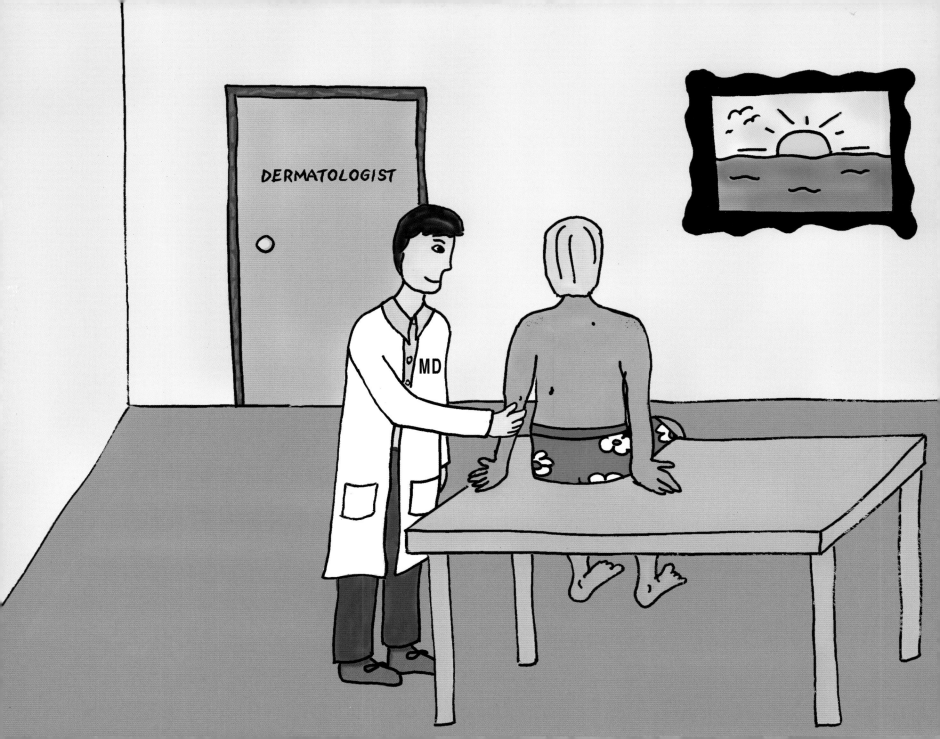

More spots on your skin?
I can think of a few,
There are moles and freckles,
And birthmarks, it's true!
But as you grow older
Become big and tall,
Just beware moles that change,
They are enemies to all.

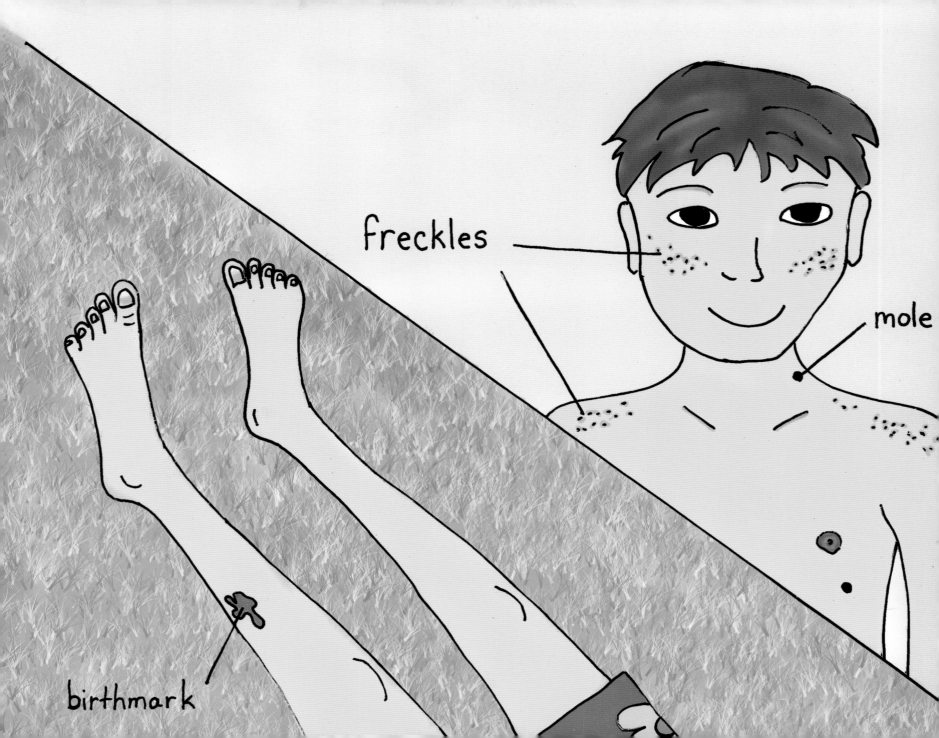

I do have some benefits
As I'm sure you can see,
I help warm the oceans
Give you Vitamin D.
And I also help gardens
And green grass to grow,
Not to mention give light
To the people below.

But let's back up
And learn about skin,
How it helps us
And keeps all our organs within.
Our skin lets us feel things
Like soft furry kittens,
Or the cold of the snow
When we don't wear our mittens.
There are also two actions
Your skin can control,
You'll sweat to cool down
And shiver when cold.

Skin varies greatly
As I'm sure that you know,
Just as freckles and hair
Help our differences show.
There's dark skin and light skin
As you may recall,
And some people
Have no pigmentation at all.

The ozone layer
Is another factor,
It protects the earth
And all of its matter.
But as it depletes
And disappears,
It leaves little protection
In our hemispheres.

After all that I've mentioned
Please protect skin,
Both when playing outdoors
And sometimes within.
Wear a hat, use an umbrella
Or stay in the shade,
But most importantly wear sunscreen!
And you'll have it made.

Watch out at the beach
When you play on the shore,
And especially in water
That's what sunscreen is for.
Because thinking you're safe
From UV's is a blunder,
They can reach you
Even when two feet under!

You may think that tanning your skin
Looks great,
But it isn't so pretty
I promise, just wait.
The results are wrinkles
And freckles and spots,
But worst, by far
Are the cancerous dots.

"Sun in a bed!" is what they say
"A tanning salon is a better way"
But tanning machines
Are really bad too.
Yes, these machines
Can cause cancer for you.
They damage the skin
Just like the sun,
And expose you to burns
Which aren't so fun.

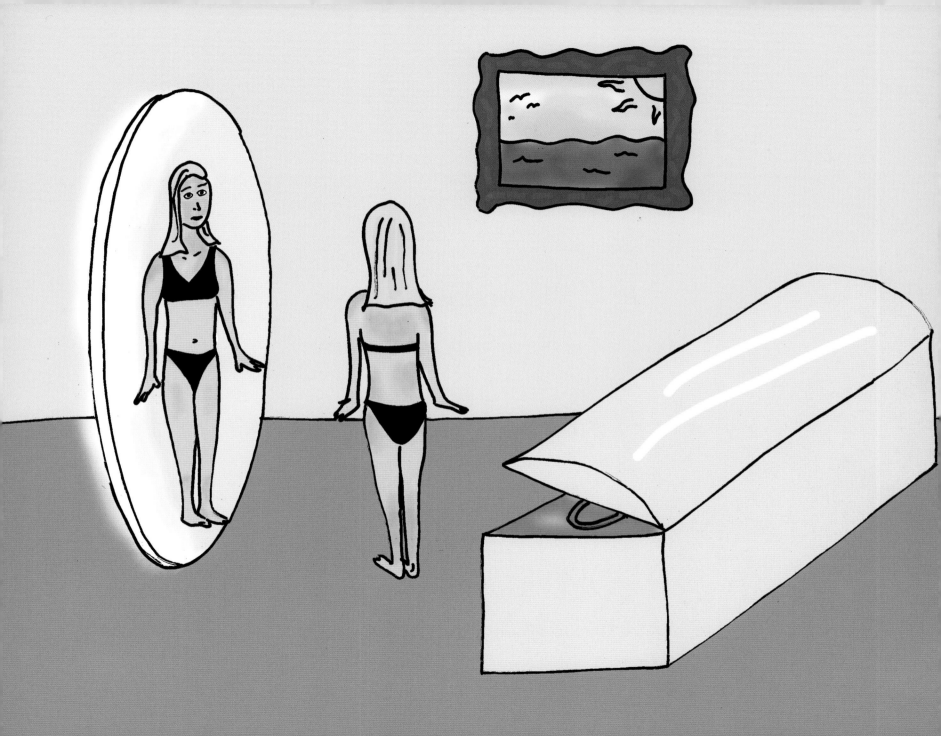

So kids,
My final advise to you
Is protect yourself,
And do spot checks too.
I may not be all bad
But beware of my rays,
And you'll safely enjoy
Those long summer days.

Fun in the Sun Safely

Dianne York-Goldman

Dianne York- Goldman, President and CEO of La Jolla Spa MD and founder of the You Glow, Girl! skin care product line, has co-authored many skin care books including *You Glow, Girl! The Ultimate Health & Skin Care Guide for Teens, Beauty Basics for Teens and the You Glow, Girl! Journal* with her husband, renound dermatologist Dr. Mitchel Goldman. Her latest children's book, **Fun in the Sun Safely** is endorsed by the American Skin Cancer Foundation and designed to give kids a fun approach to learning about how to protect themselves from the damaging effects of the sun.

Dianne is a consultant for the Girl Scouts of America and takes great pride in the education of skin care awareness, "I have learned that Beauty is a product of self esteem, which is why my company is called "You Glow Girl!" Dianne York-Goldman is a recent winner of the TWIN (Tribute to Women and Industry) award and the Women Who Mean Business awards. Her biography has appeared in Who's Who, American Executives and Professional Directories across America.

"This book was created to be a helpful tool for you and your children to have *Fun in the Sun Safely.*"

Dianne York-Goldman